METALLICA

Bass

Riff by Riff™

by Arthur Rotfeld

Photography by Ross Halfin

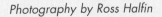

Visit our website at www.cherrylane.com

Contents

METALLICA BASSics

Metallica has always been a band unlike any other, and by the end of the sixth bar of "Hit The Lights," it is clear that we are also dealing with a bassist the likes of whom has never been heard before. Cliff Burton's formidable technique and musicianship were unrivaled by any other metal bassist of the time. (Burton was probably the fastest fingerstyle bassist to emerge since Iron Maiden's Steve Harris.) It was on *Kill 'Em All* that Burton set a new standard for heavy metal bass playing, and modern metal bassists finally had a true hero. Burton was much more than just a flashy headbanger; he was a solid ensemble player supplying the unstoppable motor drive under Hetfield's speed metal riffs, and a vital contributor to Metallica's unique sound.

Kill 'Em All is a testament to the impact Burton made in the development of the heavy metal bass. His most innovative early work, and a bounty of his trademark techniques, can be found in the epic bass solo "(Anesthesia)-Pulling Teeth." It is here that we can hear his truly individual voice, a summation of his influences—notably Jimi Hendrix, Geezer Butler, Geddy Lee, and Lemmy Kilmister—tied in with classical elements that he picked up in theory classes (evidenced by his harmonic choices, arpeggio passages, use of pedal point and various meters), all colored with hefty doses of wah and distortion. It is ironic that it took a bassist to play what is the most compelling and innovative rock instrumental since Van Halen's "Eruption."

Burton would have been a legend even if *Kill 'Em All* was his only recorded work. But on *Ride The Lightning* and *Master Of Puppets* Burton continued developing his playing style and made even more songwriting contributions. The classical tinges in "Fight Fire With Fire," "Fade To Black," and "Orion"; the distorted, wah-soaked solos in "For Whom The Bell Tolls" and the instrumental odyssey "The Call Of Ktulu"; and the relentless metal grooves in "Master Of Puppets" and "Damage, Inc." all bear the strong marks of Cliff Burton in both performance and composition.

Much like Burton did in the opening bars of "Hit The Lights," Jason Newsted gives us a good taste of his strong and innovative musical temperament in the opening bars of "Blackened," from . . . *And Justice For All*. The prevalent use of double-stops and the dark tone on this backward-recorded bass line indicate that again Metallica had a true original in the bass seat. His heavy, non-alternating pick style has added a tighter, more percussive attack to Hetfield's riffing. The endless downstrokes that he pounds out are impressive enough, but add to that the remarkable left-hand technique, evidenced in "Eye Of The Beholder" for example, and you've got a force to reckon with.

Not that chops are it for Newsted: he proves from "One" to "Until It Sleeps" that he is an imaginative and sensitive musician. His ever-evolving tone and approach, always intense and thoughtful, is present on every album—a result of his profound dedication to music and wide-ranging listening habits (everything from Sepultura to Tom Waits, Son House to Duke Ellington, Fugees to Wes Montgomery). Few bassists in the hard rock arena can lay claim to a heavier sounding track than the 5-string work he pounded out on *Metallica*'s "Sad But True," or something as haunting and dramatic as the intro he penned and played in "My Friend Of Misery." Before you're through be sure to study some of the prime characteristics of Newsted's style: for examples of his octave and double-stop playing check out "The Unforgiven," "The House Jack Built," and "Bleeding Me"; for improvisatory accompanimental grooves look to his guitar-solo backings in "The God That Failed" and "Ain't My Bitch"; also listen to his tongue-in-cheek, Flea-like thumbstyle playing in "Cure," and his inventive contrapuntal playing in "Hero Of The Day."

Cliff Burton

Cliff Burton's Gear

Basses:
Aria Pro II
Rickenbacker

Amps:
Marshall
Mesa/Boogie
Randall

Cliff Burton was born on February 10, 1962, in San Francisco. His image, ideals, and laid-back attitude came from what he described as his "hippie parents." He began playing bass in 1976, and soon after joined the local band EZ Street. When Burton's next band, Trauma, played at the Whiskey in August 1982, Lars Ulrich and James Hetfield were there. They were completely floored by Burton's playing, and Ulrich made it a full-time endeavor over the next few months to persuade him to join Metallica. Burton gave the band an ultimatum: he would join, but only if the band relocated from glam-dominated Los Angeles to San Francisco. Burton's insistence on the move to the more heavy metal–receptive Bay area was a major factor in Metallica's ensuing success. Burton's unique touches added legendary depth and character to the first three Metallica albums, *Kill 'Em All, Ride The Lightning,* and *Master Of Puppets.* His innovative playing style is widely regarded as the "next level" in heavy metal bass. Following in the tradition of Jack Bruce, Geezer Butler, and Geddy Lee, yet surpassing the considerable contributions of Lemmy Kilmister, and Steve Harris, Burton left a legacy to rock bass that will always remain . . . as solid and steady as his bass lines.

Jason Newsted

Jason Newsted's Gear

Basses:

Sadowsky 4-strings and 5-strings
Fender Precision (1958)
Spector NS (1981)

Amps:

Ampeg

Effects:

Boss Flanger, MXR Phase 100,
Mu-Tron Phasor II,
Korg G5 Bass Synth Processor,
Electro-Harmonix Big Muff

Jason Newsted uses La Bella strings
and Dunlop Tortex picks.

Jason Newsted was born on March 4, 1963, in Battle Creek, Michigan. His first experience with music was playing saxophone in the junior high school band. In his early teens, Newsted became interested in the bass after hearing Gene Simmons play in Kiss. He persuaded his father to give him a bass as his 14th birthday present, though he didn't take playing seriously until he was 18. It was at this time that Newsted traveled west, heading for California, but when the funds ran out he found himself in Arizona working two jobs to pay for a "cool bass and rig." Shortly thereafter he helped form Flotsam and Jetsam and was soon playing every major club in the Arizona area. They released the album *Doomsday For The Deceiver* on Metal Blade Records in 1986. Highly recommended for the Metallica bass throne, empty after Burton's tragic death on September 27, 1986, Newsted was one of 40 musicians who auditioned, including Kirk Hammett's friend, and soon-to-be Primus bassist, Les Claypool. Eleven days after the audition, Newsted was on tour as Metallica's new bassist. Newsted's thunderous sound and impeccable musical judgment have graced every album since.

Hit The Lights

from KILL 'EM ALL

Words and Music by James Hetfield and Lars Ulrich

Dramatic Intro

Here Burton assaults us with his impressive *tremolo* (the quick and continuous reiteration of a single pitch, shown as ≡ in the music). The tremolos—and the 32nd-note passage—are executed using alternate strokes with the first and second fingers of the right hand.

0:00

Intro Riff

This line fills out the bottom end of Hetfield's lean and mean guitar part. Note that when Hetfield plays the double-stop 4ths, Burton doubles the *top* note (two octaves lower), thus splitting a power chord (root-fifth-octave) between the bass and guitar.

0:47

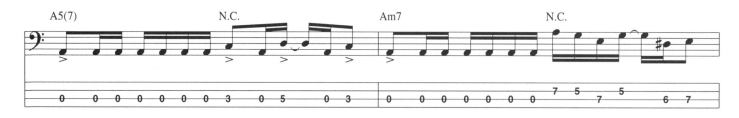

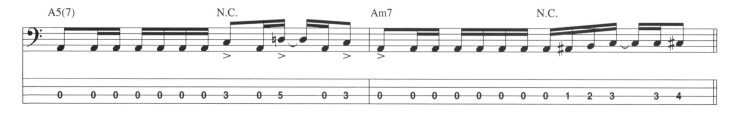

The Four Horsemen

from KILL 'EM ALL

Words and Music by James Hetfield and Lars Ulrich and Dave Mustaine
Copyright © 1983 Creeping Death Music (ASCAP)
This Arrangement Copyright © 1990 by Creeping Death Music
International Copyright Secured All Rights Reserved

Verse Riff

The racing triplets on beats 1 and 3 and the strong accents on beats 2 and 4 give this riff its rhythmic impetus.

0:17

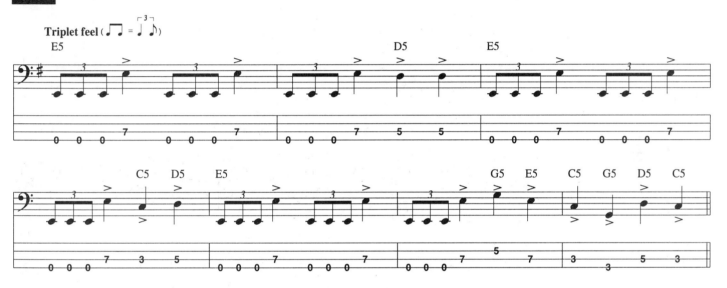

Turn The Beat Around

This riff, from the bridge, is based on the triplet figure from the previous riff, only now it is "turned around"; in other words, the triplets fall on beats 2 and 4, and the strong accents are now on beats 1 and 3. Notice the way that it tugs and pulls against Ulrich's relentless back-beat (accents on beats 2 and 4) groove.

2:13

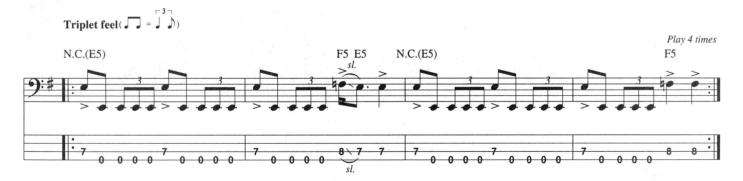

The Four Horsemen (Cont.)

Geezer Would Be Proud

This bluesy, transitional riff is played at ♩=102—half the tempo of the previous example. Much like Black Sabbath's blues scale triplet riffs, Burton doubles the guitar figure (in E: E G A B♭ B D) an octave lower, à la Geezer Butler.

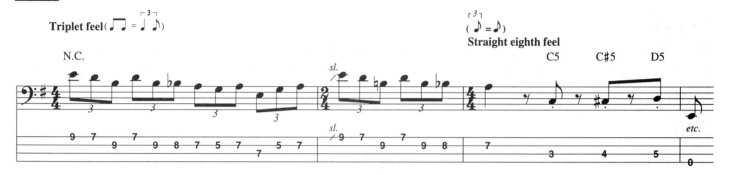

Contrary Motion Riff

Notice the climbing effect of Burton's line in this section preceding the guitar solo. While the guitars sink into lower and lower voicings, the bass line rises, in contrary motion, until, in the final bars, it is actually higher than the guitar part. (If your bass has only 20 frets, play the G and B in the last bar on the 12th and 16th frets [respectively] of the G string.)

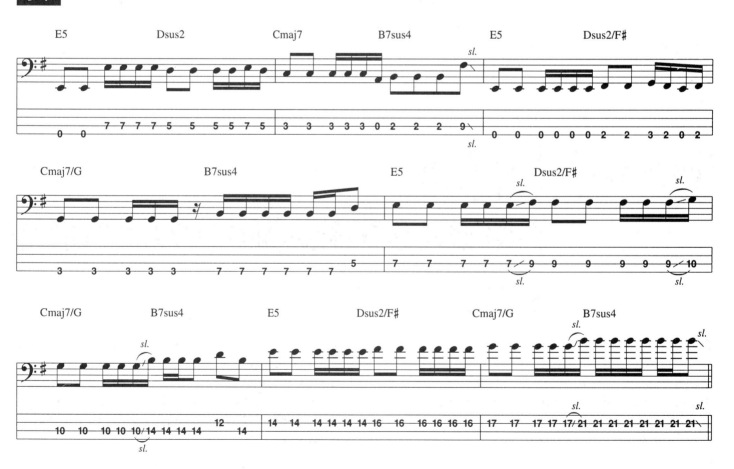

Motorbreath

from *KILL 'EM ALL*

Words and Music by James Hetfield
Copyright © 1983 Creeping Death Music (ASCAP)
This Arrangement Copyright © 1990 by Creeping Death Music
International Copyright Secured All Rights Reserved

Verse Riff

If you listen closely to this figure you'll notice subtle rhythmic differences between the bass, guitar, and drums. Compare the guitar's rhythm (♪♩ ♪♫ ♫) to the bass's rhythm to see how Burton reinforces, yet contrasts, the guitar part.

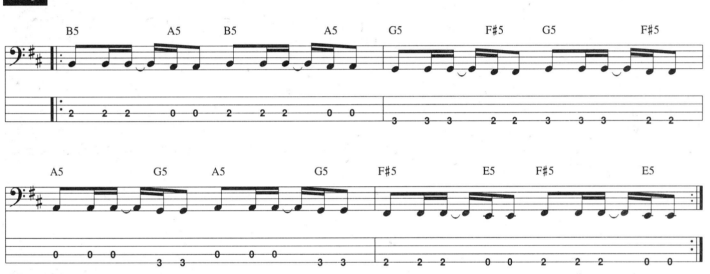

(Anesthesia)-Pulling Teeth

from *KILL 'EM ALL*

Music by Cliff Burton
Copyright © 1983 Creeping Death Music (ASCAP)
This Arrangement Copyright © 1990 by Creeping Death Music
International Copyright Secured All Rights Reserved

Far too long to be considered a riff, yet far too important to be left out of a book like this—after all, this is probably the bass player's "Eruption." Even though it's not quite as flashy as Eddie Van Halen's guitar extravaganza, the development of ideas and use of tone color in "(Anesthesia)-Pulling Teeth" is quite sophisticated, perhaps harking back to Hendrix's version of "The Star Spangled Banner." Go visit a guitar-playing friend and ask to borrow his distortion pedal and wah—you'll need both for this piece. The distortion allows Burton to achieve a thick, overtone-rich sound, while the wah is used for some extreme-sounding dramatic effects.

(Anesthesia)- Pulling Teeth (Cont.)

0:00

* o = open (bass)
+ = closed (treble)

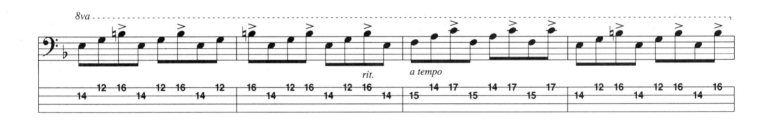

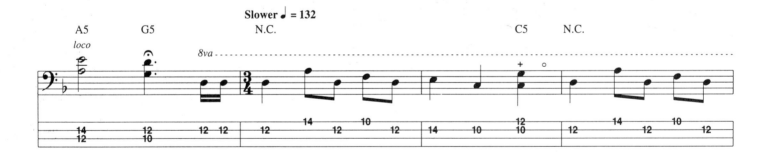

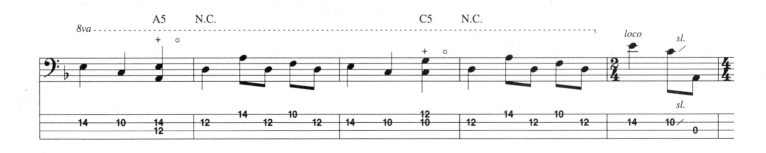

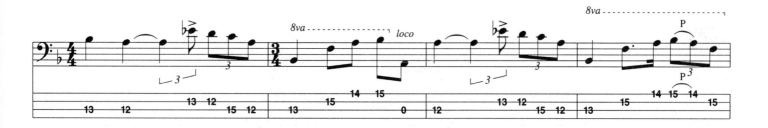

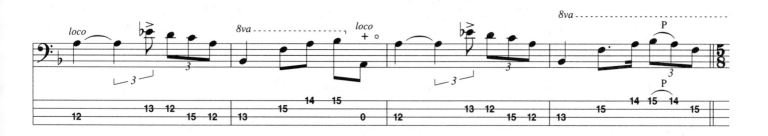

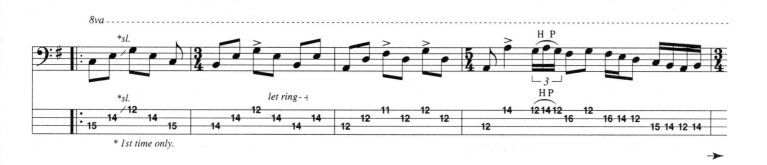

* 1st time only.

(Anesthesia)-Pulling Teeth (Cont.)

(Anesthesia)-Pulling Teeth (Cont.)

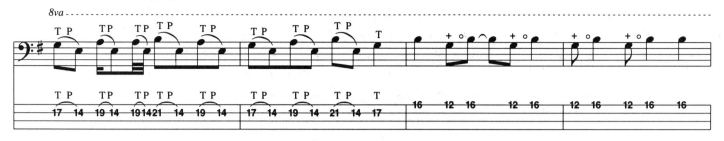

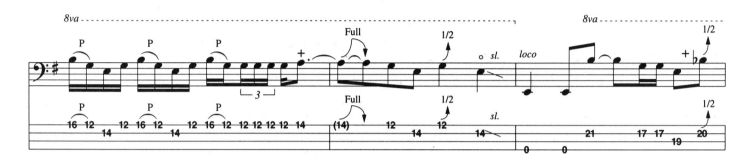

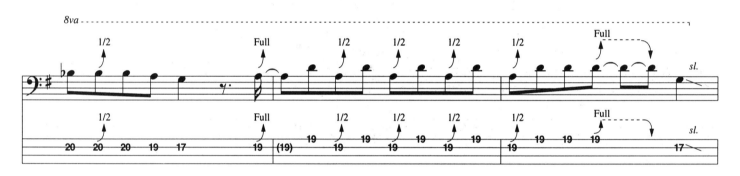

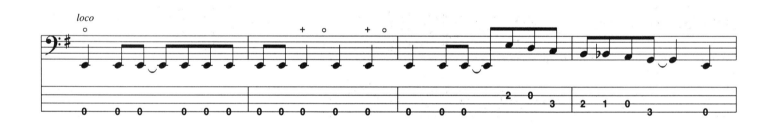

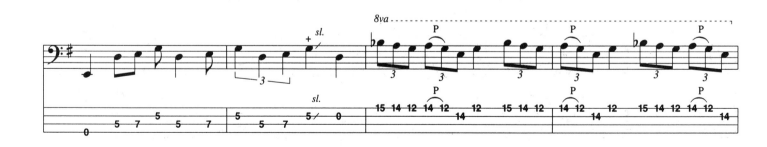

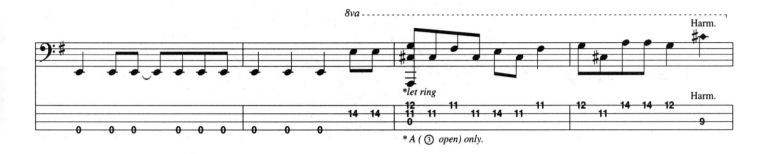

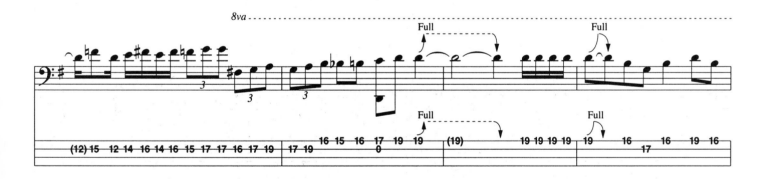

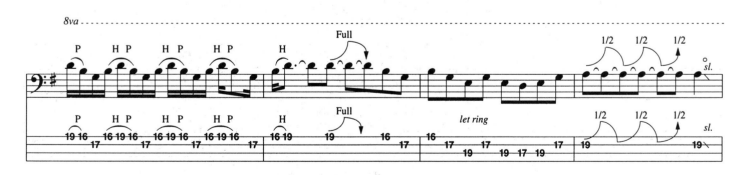

(Anesthesia)-Pulling Teeth (Cont.)

* Drag R.H. nails along ** Tap open D and G strings against pickup in rhythm indicated.   *** Nail scrape
E and A strings starting
at 1st fret.

Phantom Lord

from KILL 'EM ALL

Words and Music by James Hetfield, Lars Ulrich and Dave Mustaine
Copyright © 1983 Creeping Death Music (ASCAP)
This Arrangement Copyright © 1990 by Creeping Death Music
International Copyright Secured All Rights Reserved

Verse Riff

This riff will serve as a great string-skipping exercise. Pluck the highest E, in the two-octave figure with your middle finger, and play the rest with alternating index- and middle-finger strokes.

0:50

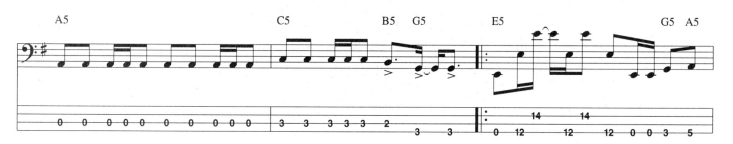

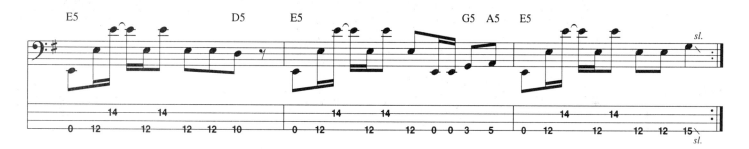

Chorus Riff

Though it appears that this phrase begins with the downbeat E, it really starts on the A that immediately follows it, and *ends* on the downbeat E of the ensuing bar.

1:09

Seek & Destroy

from *KILL 'EM ALL*

Words and Music by James Hetfield and Lars Ulrich

Verse Riff

The moderate tempo of this song makes this riff easy to play. Note that the end of each two-bar phrase contains the same notes (B–B♭–G–E); variety is achieved through the octave displacement of the G and E.

0:56

Fight Fire With Fire

from RIDE THE LIGHTNING

Words and Music by James Hetfield, Lars Ulrich and Cliff Burton

Intro Riff

Burton plays almost all of this infectious melodic line in the 9th position (1st finger on the 9th fret, 2nd finger on the 10th fret, etc.) The final lick requires a jump to 12th position.

0:00

For Whom The Bell Tolls

from RIDE THE LIGHTNING

Words and Music by James Hetfield, Lars Ulrich and Cliff Burton

Guitaristic Intro Riff

The upstemmed part shown below is another example of Burton's use of wah and distortion to give himself a guitar-like tone. Burton doesn't play the upstemmed and downstemmed part at the same time—the upper line was overdubbed. P.S. Don't let some guitarist talk you into playing the only the downstemmed part—this is your turn to shine!

0:00

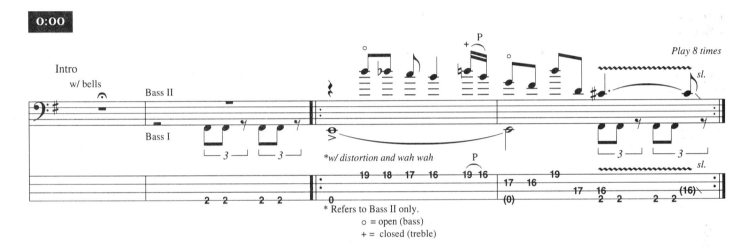

* Refers to Bass II only.
o = open (bass)
+ = closed (treble)

Eighth-Note Riff

If this riff included the pinkie it would be a classic finger exercise. Even though the pinkie isn't used, the constant motion, low position, and incorporation of three fingers make this riff a good warm-up—yet musical—exercise.

0:57

Fade To Black

from RIDE THE LIGHTNING

Words and Music by James Hetfield, Lars Ulrich, Cliff Burton and Kirk Hammett
Copyright © 1984 Creeping Death Music (ASCAP)
This Arrangement Copyright © 1990 by Creeping Death Music
International Copyright Secured All Rights Reserved

Verse Riff

Though the verses are composed of a repeated chord progression (Am–C–G–Em), Burton was not a come-up-with-a-pattern-and-stick-with-it kind of bass player; he devised with many ways to weave through this progression. Compare and contrast Burton's four phrases in this 16-bar verse. His endings of phrases (bars 4, 8, 12, and 16) show the most variation.

1:57

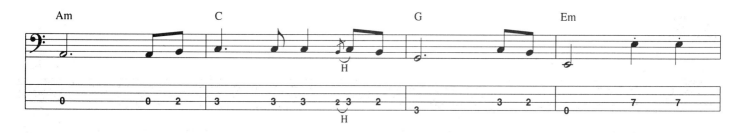

Fade To Black (Cont.)

Bridge Riff

The first three bars of this riff closely follow the vocal line. The final bar's descending figure, played in the gallop rhythm, functions as a *turnaround,* which is a short riff or progression that leads back to the beginning of the entire riff or progression.

3:53

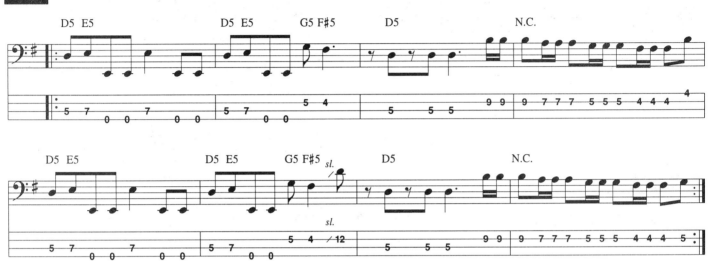

The Call Of Ktulu

from *RIDE THE LIGHTNING*

Words and Music by James Hetfield, Lars Ulrich, Cliff Burton and Dave Mustaine
Copyright © 1984 Creeping Death Music (ASCAP)
This Arrangement Copyright © 1990 by Creeping Death Music
International Copyright Secured All Rights Reserved

Bass Solo

Burton's solo is unfortunately somewhat buried in the mix, but with some careful EQ adjustments on your stereo you can bring out his part a bit more. As usual, he colors his tone with distortion and wah. His use of the wah, especially the treble boosts, contributes to the mysterious and sinister mood. The artificial harmonics in bar 4 are played using right-hand taps, *directly* on top of the 10th fret, while still holding the 6th fret D♯ with the left hand.

1:28

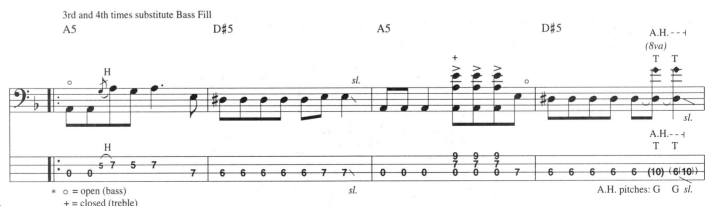

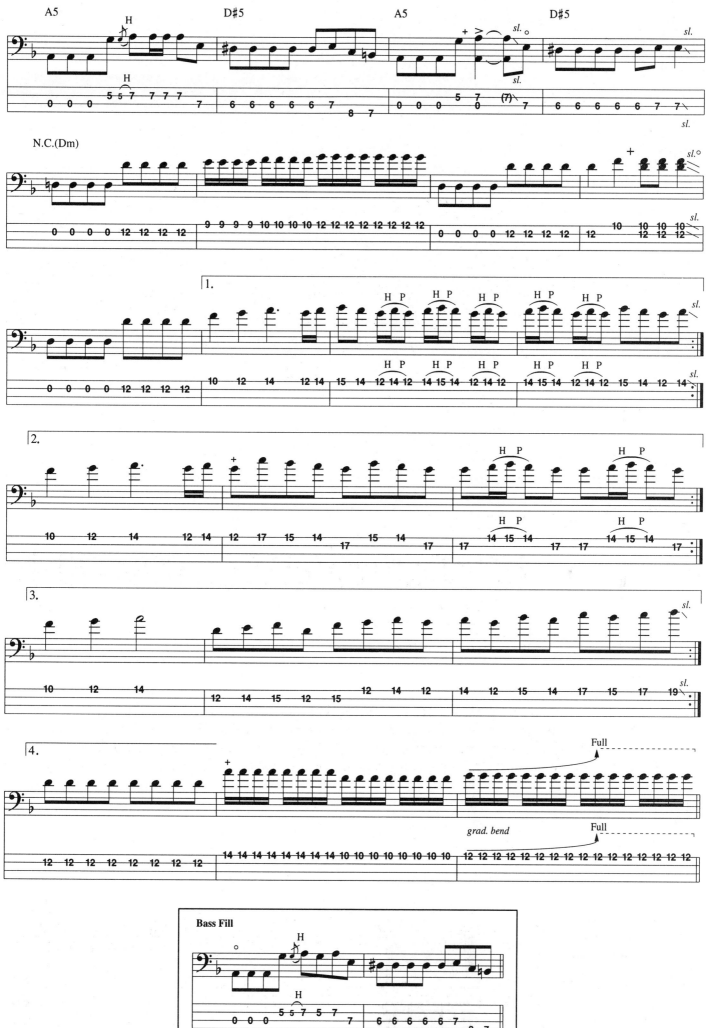

Battery

from *MASTER OF PUPPETS*

Words and Music by James Hetfield and Lars Ulrich
Copyright © 1986 Creeping Death Music (ASCAP)
This Arrangement Copyright © 1988 by Creeping Death Music
International Copyright Secured All Rights Reserved

Intro Riff

Burton's line in this slow and powerful section is reinforced by hits from Ulrich's bass drums.

Verse Riff

Here, Burton fills out the bottom end with the obligatory heavy metal gallop rhythm. The combination of Ulrich's off-beat snare hits and Burton's chugging bass line gives this song its driving and relentless groove.

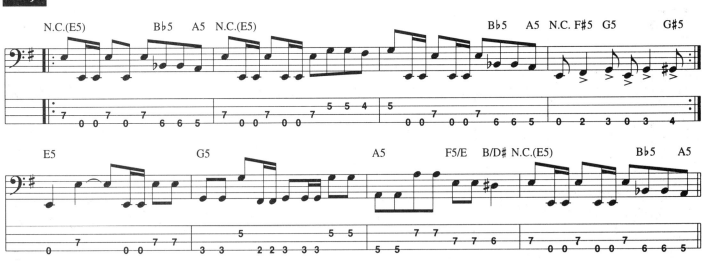

Master Of Puppets

from MASTER OF PUPPETS

Words and Music by James Hetfield, Lars Ulrich, Kirk Hammett and Cliff Burton

Intro Riff #1

Burton accents each note in this riff, which is played in unison with Hetfield's chords and Ulrich's choked cymbal crashes.

0:00

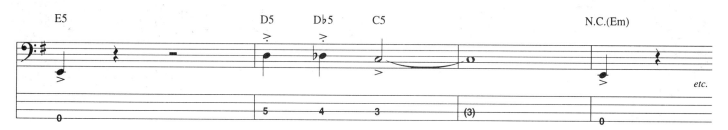

Intro Riff #2

This riff will serve as a good exercise for finger stretches. Play it in 1st position and be sure to use your pinkie for the C♯ on the 4th fret of the A string.

0:30

Master Of Puppets (Cont.)

Verse Riff

Play this riff in 3rd position; use your 4th finger for the slide in bar 2, but use your first finger for the slide in bar 4.

1:01

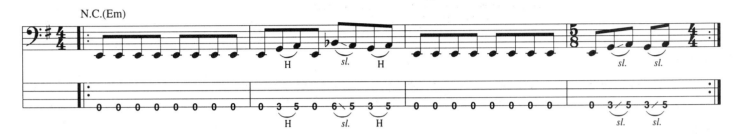

Pre-Chorus Riff

The half-time feel of this riff provides a somewhat calmer mood.

1:32

Interlude Riff

A tranquil mood prevails in this section. The riff shown below is played, with slight variations, throughout this interlude section.

3:52

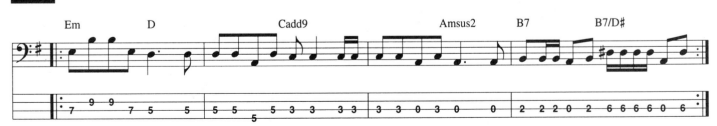

The Thing That Should Not Be

from *MASTER OF PUPPETS*

Words and Music by James Hetfield and Lars Ulrich and Kirk Hammett

Intro Riff

This riff is composed of a three-note chromatic motive, first heard at the outset as E–F–F♯, and then, above the low F♯ pedal, as C–C♯–D. Begin this riff in 1st position, but switch to 2nd position on beat 4 of the first bar.

0:17

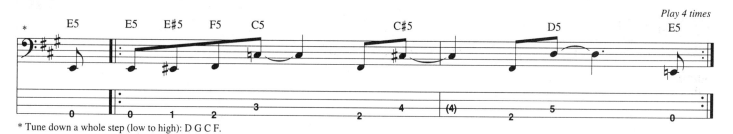

* Tune down a whole step (low to high): D G C F.

Sequential Riff

This riff is a sequence of a short melodic pattern, or motive, played on the lowest string.

0:43

* Tune down a whole step (low to high): D G C F.

Welcome Home (Sanitarium)

from *MASTER OF PUPPETS*

Words and Music by James Hetfield, Lars Ulrich and Kirk Hammett
Copyright © 1986 Creeping Death Music (ASCAP)
This Arrangement Copyright © 1988 by Creeping Death Music
International Copyright Secured All Rights Reserved

Intro/Verse Riff

The eighth notes on beats 2½ and 4½ give this riff a strong sense of forward momentum.

Chorus Riff

The notes shown as **x**'s represent muted notes; they can be played by lightly dampening the string with your left hand's middle finger, which will be used to finger the pitched notes that follow.

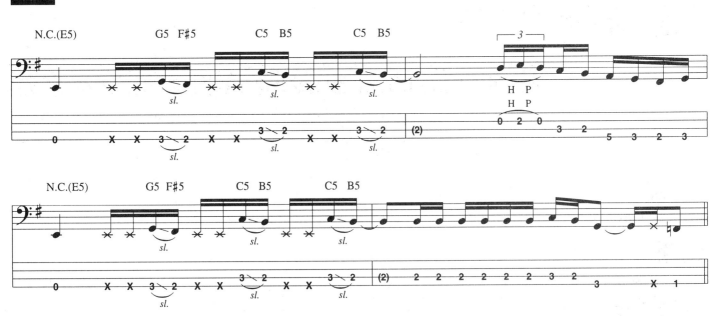

Bridge Riff

This riff is based almost entirely on a ♫♩ rhythm. A surprising Phrygian (1 ♭2 ♭3 4 5 ♭6 ♭7) sound occurs in bar 3, when the F5 chord (♭II in E), appears.

Disposable Heroes

from *MASTER OF PUPPETS*

Words and Music by James Hetfield, Lars Ulrich and Kirk Hammett

Intro Riff

This fast intro riff proves that it is possible to be ultra-heavy and totally thrashy in 6/4.

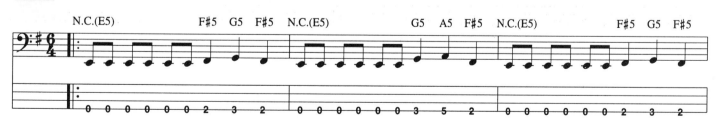

Disposable Heroes (Cont.)

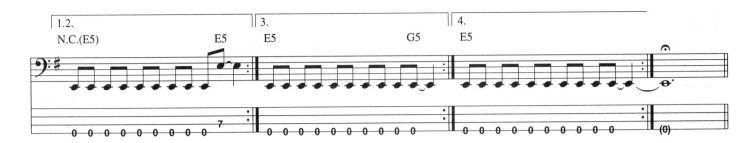

Leper Messiah

from MASTER OF PUPPETS

Words and Music by James Hetfield and Lars Ulrich

Intro Riff

This riff relies on staccato articulations and other short, punctuated notes for its stumbling and staggering effect.

0:18

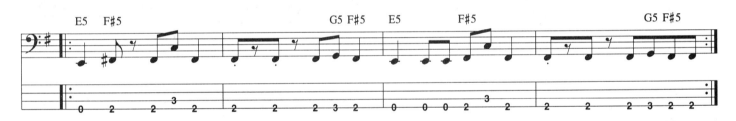

Verse Riff

This riff, like the Intro Riff, makes important use of the E5 and F#5 chords. Notice the accents on beats 1 and 3, which not only conflict with Ulrich's back-beat groove, but also contrast with the 2 and 4 accents of the Intro Riff.

1:00

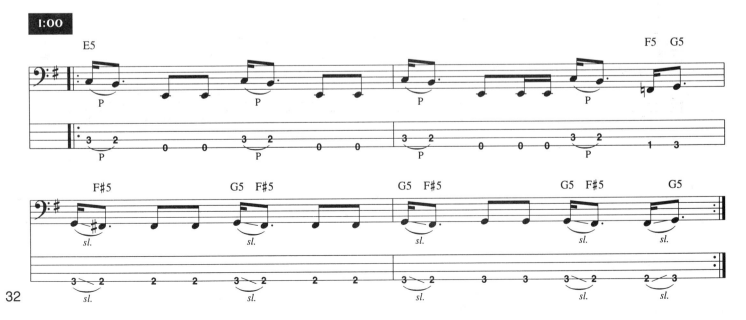

Chorus Riff

Based on the ♫. ♫ rhythm of the Verse Riff, this figure unfolds in a series of descending fretted notes above a low E pedal.

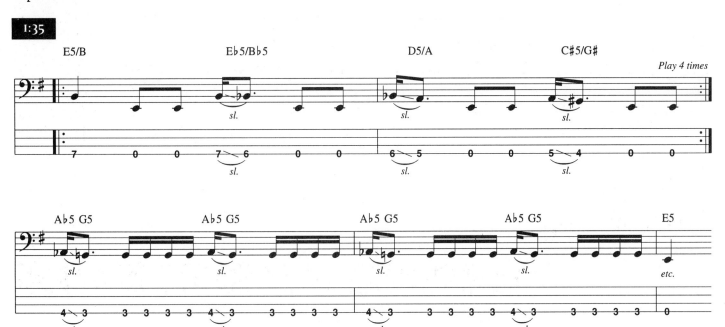

Orion

Odd-Grouping Riff

In this riff the guitars and bass conflict with Ulrich's straight-forward, $\frac{4}{4}$ playing. Though notated in $\frac{4}{4}$, this riff sounds more like $\frac{3+3+2}{8}$. (You can count it as either 1-&-2-&-3-&-4-& or 1-2-3-4-5-6-7-8.)

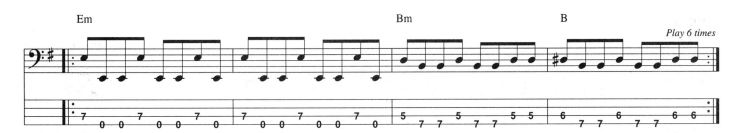

Orion (Cont.)

Pedal-Point Riff

Similar to the Chorus Riff in "Leper Messiah," this riff is composed of a low E pedal, only now the melodic line above the pedal point has an arch-like contour.

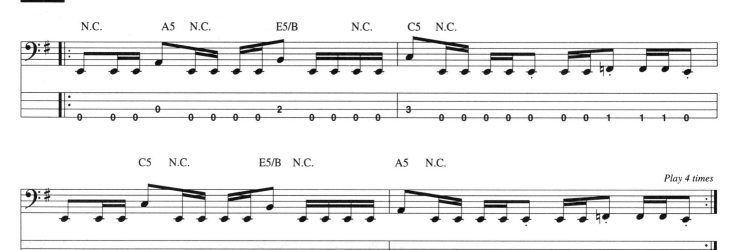

§ Riff

It is likely that this section, with its prominent bass line, was written by Burton, as it recalls similar parts in "(Anesthesia)-Pulling Teeth." The § meter adds to the classical feel of this riff, and is reminiscent of the *gigue*, a Baroque dance in § time. Burton always varies the end of each phrase (bars 8, 16, and 20) to increase interest *and* momentum, in what otherwise would have been a repetitious, pattern-oriented riff.

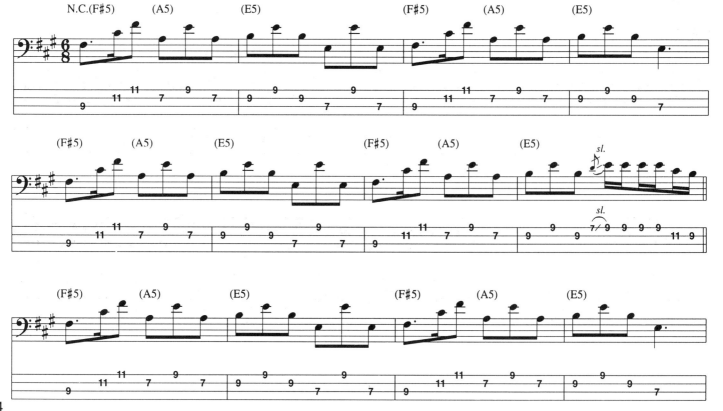

Damage, Inc.

from MASTER OF PUPPETS

Words and Music by James Hetfield, Lars Ulrich, Kirk Hammett and Cliff Burton

Sixteenth-Note Riff

At ♩=190, this riff is a tough one. If you have difficulty with fast, sixteenth-note riffs, you'll need practice with a metronome. (Don't try to "meet" the metronome; instead, set it at a tempo you are already comfortable with, and gradually increase the speed over an extended period of time—it may take several days, weeks, or even months before your fingers can handle sixteenth notes at these blinding tempos.) Remember, always play sixteenth-note passages with alternating first- and second-finger strokes.

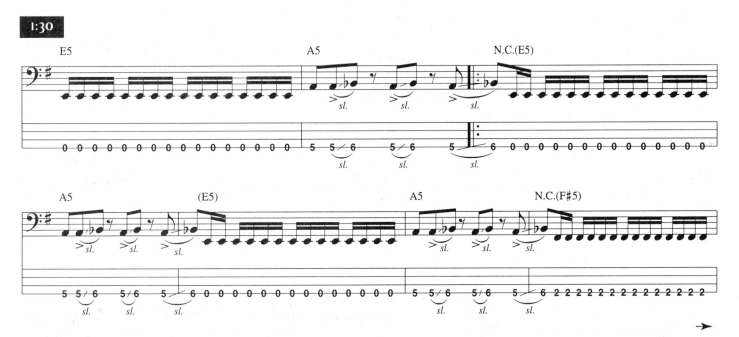

Damage, Inc. (Cont.)

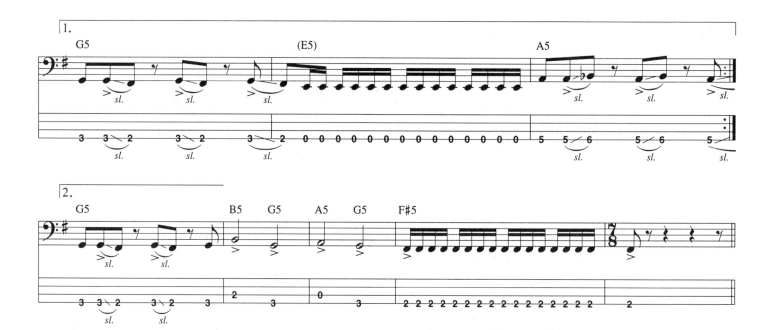

Blackened

from ... *AND JUSTICE FOR ALL*

Words and Music by James Hetfield, Lars Ulrich and Jason Newsted
Copyright © 1988 Creeping Death Music (ASCAP)
This Arrangement Copyright © 1989 by Creeping Death Music
International Copyright Secured All Rights Reserved

Backwards Intro Riff

Newsted's bass line for this intro is backwards. In other words, the riff was actually recorded beginning in the last bar and ending in the first. Notice the prevalent double-stops (in every second bar), an important facet in Newsted's playing.

0:00

* Backwards bass guitar

$\frac{7}{4}$ Riff

This riff, with its irregular phrase length (seven beats) and frequent ♭5's (B♭) and ♭2's (F♮), has a frantic and unsettling sound.

Verse Riff

Born from the previous riff, this more symmetrical version, in $\frac{6}{4}$, also makes use of repeated E's (albeit without octave displacements) and the always-popular tritone relationship (E–B♭).

Chorus Riff

The octave E double-stops from the intro return here, at the outset of the chorus. Newsted gets a tight and punchy sound from his pickstyle playing; notice his perfect synchronization with Ulrich in bars 4 and 8.

...And Justice For All

from ... AND JUSTICE FOR ALL

Words and Music by James Hetfield, Lars Ulrich and Kirk Hammett

Intro Riff

Even though this riff is as heavy as can be, it's composed of nothing more than notes from the E blues scale (E G A B♭ B♮ D). A sense of urgency is created in bar 3 by incorporating a truncated version of the first bar.

Pre-Chorus Riff

This riff is straight-ahead until the final bar, when those flying triplets come out of nowhere! Newsted gets a real kick out of playing these kinds of virtuosic figures with the guitars.

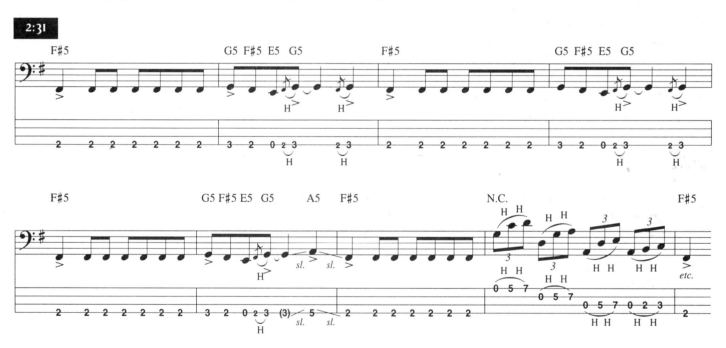

Eye Of The Beholder

from ... AND JUSTICE FOR ALL

Words and Music by James Hetfield, Lars Ulrich and Kirk Hammett

Intro Riff

The most difficult thing about this riff is recognizing where the downbeat is. You might get a false sense of the "one" from the guitars, which accent beat 4½. You may find it helpful—and grounding—to know that when Ulrich's snare-drum hits enter they are on beat 3.

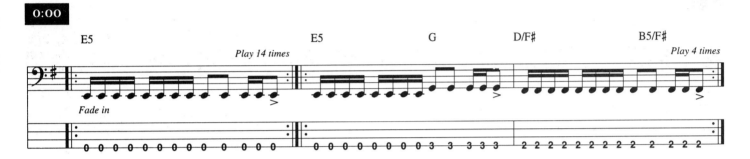

Second Intro Riff

To achieve contrast with the previous riff, Newsted uses octave leaps (instead of using an E in only one register) for added variety and interest. The fiendish, trill-like figure at the end of this riff (again, played along with the guitars) can be executed in two ways. First (this *is* cheating, by the way), play each figure with the first and second fingers of the left hand, which necessitates switching positions on each beat, but it's easy on the hand, as it avoids the use of the 3rd and 4th fingers. Second, for you chops-meisters out there, play the first three groups of sixteenth notes in 6th position—the "proper" way to finger this passage. This also gives your left hand a challenging exercise that will develop strength and accuracy in your weaker fingers. The final group—regardless of the method—is played in 2nd position.

39

Eye Of The Beholder (Cont.)

¹²⁄₈ Riff

This is the odd-grouped ¹²⁄₈ riff from the pre-chorus. Notice the unusual, syncopated accent pattern, **1**-**2**-3-**4**-5-**6**-**7**-8-9-**10**-11-**12** instead of the more typical **1**-2-3-**4**-5-6-**7**-8-9-**10**-11-12.

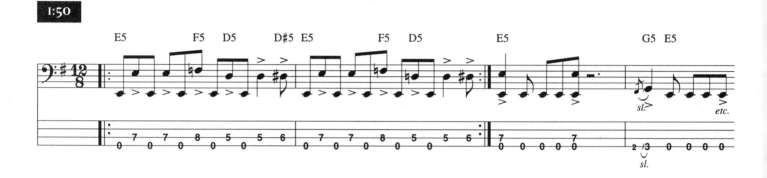

One

from ... AND JUSTICE FOR ALL

Words and Music by James Hetfield and Lars Ulrich

Verse Riff #1

Newsted's bass line, filled with a wide variety of rhythms and fills, invigorates the song during the verses.

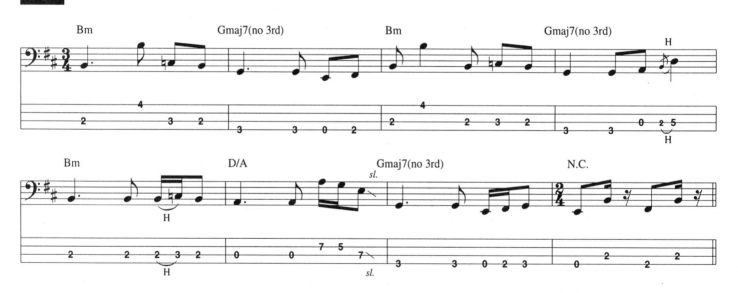

"One" continued on page 45

One (Cont.)

Verse Riff #2

This riff thickens the texture by matching the vocal line ("Hold my breath as I wish for death.") in the first bar.

2:13

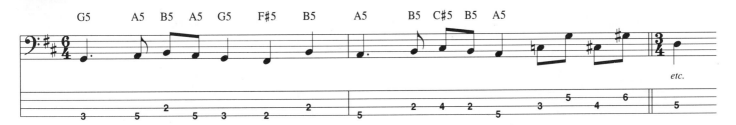

Sixteenth-Note-Triplet Riff

This terrifying riff is banged out with relentless tenacity. All of the remaining riffs in this song are based on this riff.

4:37

The Shortest Straw

from ... AND JUSTICE FOR ALL

Words and Music by James Hetfield and Lars Ulrich

Intro Riff #1

Some of Hetfield's favorite chords, E5 (i), F5 (♭II), G5 (III), and B♭5 (♭V), reign throughout this riff. Though the guitars play many syncopations, Newsted lays it down, placing notes on every beat, establishing a firm ground.

0:13

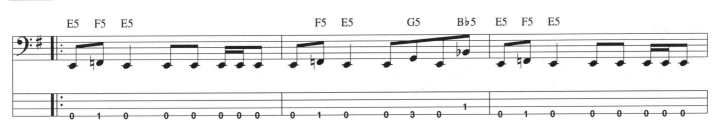

The Shortest Straw (Cont.)

Intro Riff #2

Newsted plays this figure under Hetfield's evil, tritone-laden riff. The way that this riff matches up with the guitar every time Hetfield plays an A or B♭ is particularly effective.

0:52

Verse Riff

Using many of the same chords as in the intro, Hetfield achieves contrast here by adopting a new—and highly syncopated—rhythm. Newsted doubles the lowest notes of the guitar part, an octave below, throughout this riff.

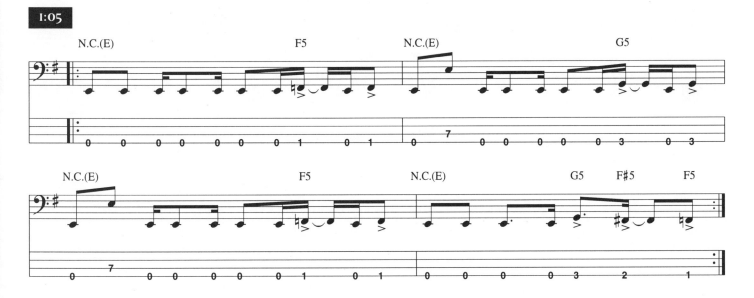

Harvester Of Sorrow

from ... *AND JUSTICE FOR ALL*

Words and Music by James Hetfield and Lars Ulrich

Intro Riff #1

The entire band plays this figure together, for utmost power and vigor. Even though it appears to be a simple and even sixteenth-note figure, there is an implied syncopation imparted by the groupings in threes.

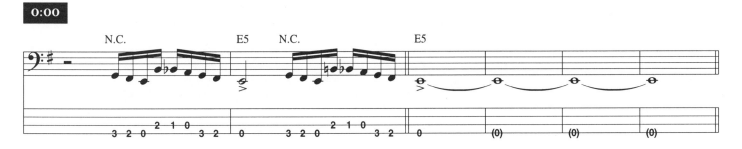

Harvester Of Sorrow (Cont.)

Intro Riff #2

This is simply a more fleshed out version of Intro Riff #1: the placement of the sixteenth-note figure is identical, only now it is surrounded by E's and F's in the gallop rhythm.

Verse Riff

The slow tempo of this song (♩=84) will enable you to easily play all of the eighth-note figures with downstrokes. The downstrokes are necessary for the heavy accents on the "and" of each beat.

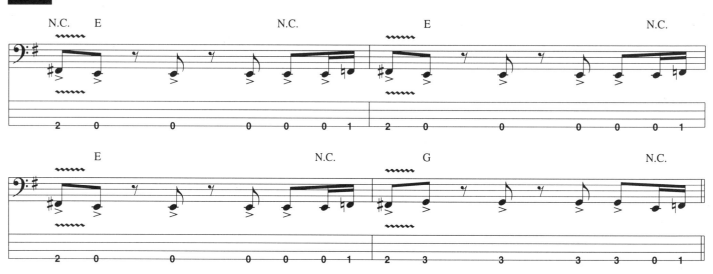

The Frayed Ends Of Sanity

from ... And Justice For All

Words and Music by James Hetfield, Lars Ulrich and Kirk Hammett

"Wizard of Oz" Riff

Newsted gets a heavy and dark tone by playing the B♭ on the 6th fret of the 4th string, instead of on the 1st fret of the lighter A string. Try playing it both ways, paying close attention to the timbral differences.

0:09

Pre-Verse Riff

This riff is played in 1st position, mainly to facilitate the notes that occur on beat 4. The sixteenth-note rests in this riff are "played" by quickly resting your right-hand fingers on the string to prevent the note from sounding.

0:42

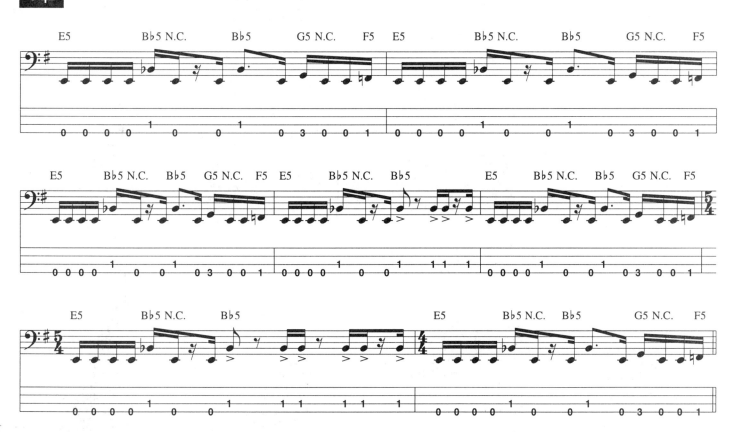

The Frayed Ends Of Sanity (Cont.)

Double-Stop Riff

This riff, played during the verses, is a prime example of Newsted's double-stop technique. The top note of each of these double-stops is present in the guitar part, but the lower note is foreign to the guitar's chords; this relationship is reflected in the chord names.

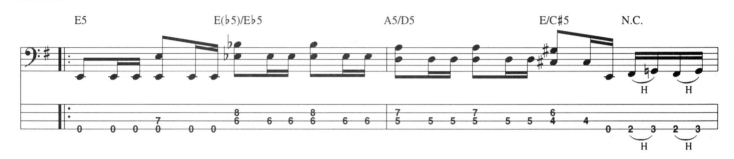

To Live Is To Die

from ... AND JUSTICE FOR ALL

Words and Music by James Hetfield, Lars Ulrich and Cliff Burton

Copyright © 1988 Creeping Death Music (ASCAP)
This Arrangement Copyright © 1989 by Creeping Death Music
International Copyright Secured All Rights Reserved

Motivic Riff

This entire riff is composed of a four-note motive (F#–G–F#–A). In the first four bars, the motive is spread out, essentially one note per bar (not including the less structurally significant neighbor tones, such as the E in the first bar). The compositional technique of *diminution* is applied three times in the final bars of this riff; i.e., the rhythmic value of the motive is halved in each successive bar. Diminution is a commonly used device in classical pieces.

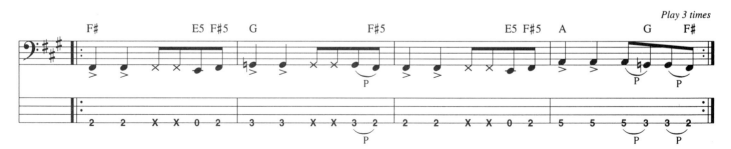

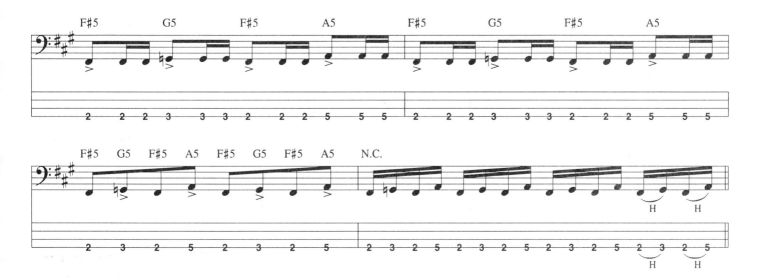

Dyers Eve

from ... AND JUSTICE FOR ALL

Words and Music by James Hetfield, Lars Ulrich and Kirk Hammett

Alternating 4/4 and 3/4 Riff

Before you attempt this riff, try counting along with the recording to get a sense of the rhythmic flow of these meter changes. The stresses are on the strong beats: **1**-2-**3**-4, **1**-2-**3**.

`0:00`

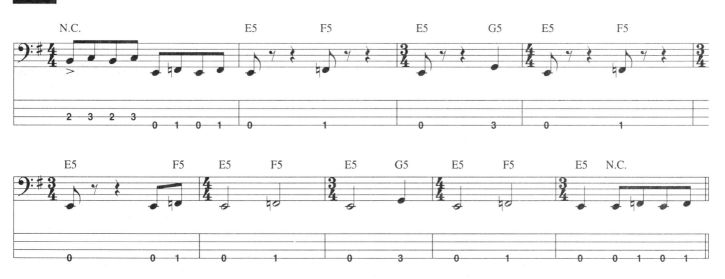

Dyers Eve (Cont.)

Second Intro Riff

This part of the intro (just after the decelerating drum fill) makes a temporary move from the previous E Phrygian (E F G A B C D) sound to a B Phrygian (B C D E F♯ G A) sound.

0:36

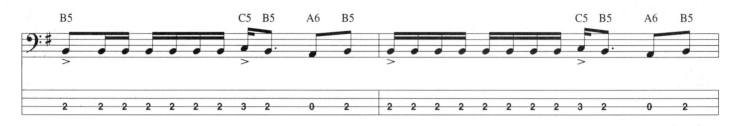

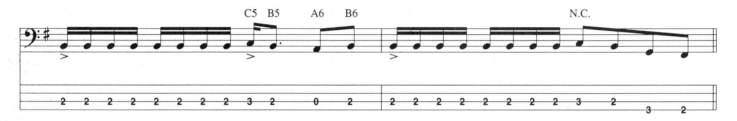

Verse Riff

This riff uses the rhythm known, in heavy metal circles, as the reverse gallop (♪♪♩ ♪♪♩). Notice the use of the low E pedal.

1:12

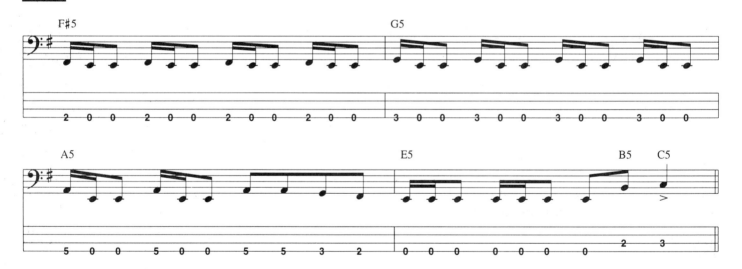

Enter Sandman

from METALLICA

Words and Music by James Hetfield, Lars Ulrich and Kirk Hammett

Intro/Verse Riff

This simple, all-eighth-note riff is used in the intro and again later in the verses. The F♮ placed on beat 4½ in many of these bars gives the groove a push.

0:24

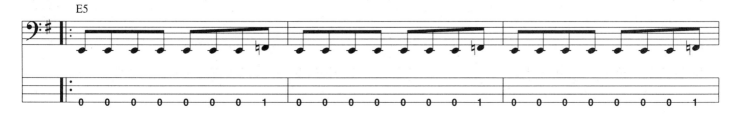

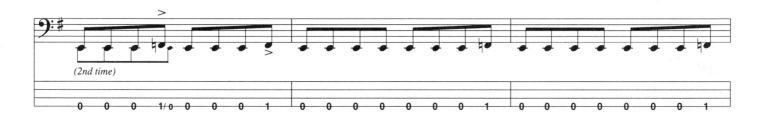

Second Intro Riff

This riff is based closely on the guitar riff that is played above it. Newsted fills in some of the space left open in the guitar, by playing an almost constant, heavy eighth-note part.

0:55

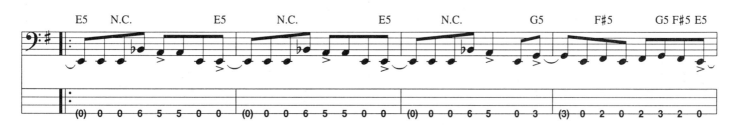

Enter Sandman (Cont.)

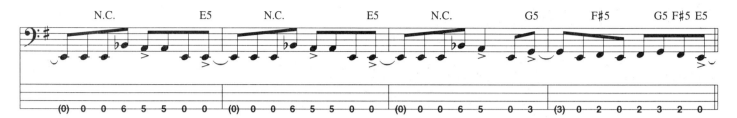

Chorus Riff

The riff used in the chorus begins with a transposition of the Second Intro Riff (up a whole step). Take the slide in bar 4 with your third finger, thus placing you in 5th position. Come back down to 2nd position at the end of the bar by playing the G♮ (3rd fret of the E string) with your second finger.

Sad But True

from METALLICA

Words and Music by James Hetfield and Lars Ulrich

Intro Riff #1

This may be truly sad for those of you with four-string basses: Newsted uses a five-string bass (tuned down a whole step) on this song. (Note that the standard notation and chord names are notated as if the instrument has *not* been tuned down a whole step.) By tuning down a perfect 5th (3½ steps) your can approximate his sound, but when strings are loosened this much they can sound floppy and loose, so you might want to try the bottom four strings from a five-string set for a more satisfying sound.

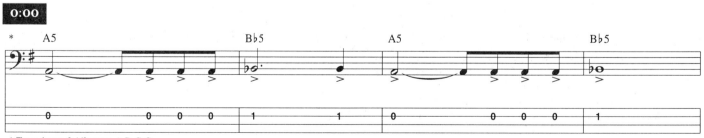

* Tune down 3 1/2 steps: A D G C.

(This tuning simulates the bottom 4 strings of a 5-stg. bass, tuned down one whole step. For best results, instrument should be re-strung.)

Intro Riff #2

Newsted thickens the already massive sound by playing octave E's in the opening of this riff.

`0:22`

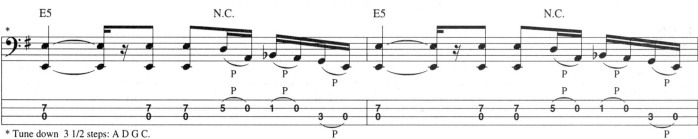

* Tune down 3 1/2 steps: A D G C.
  (This tuning simulates the bottom 4 strings of a 5-stg. bass, tuned down one whole step. For best results, instrument should be re-strung.)

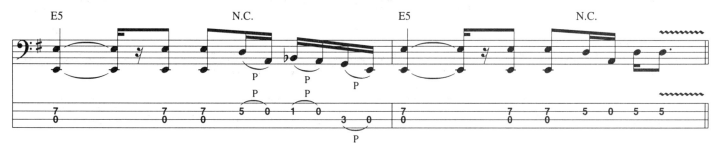

Chorus Riff

The beginning of this riff is composed primarily of an E pedal, ornamented by notes from the E Phrygian mode (E F G A B C D). The triplet hits in the final bar are played by the entire band. As the only triplets in the song, they noticeably contrast all of the other rhythms (composed of eighth and sixteenth notes).

`1:16`

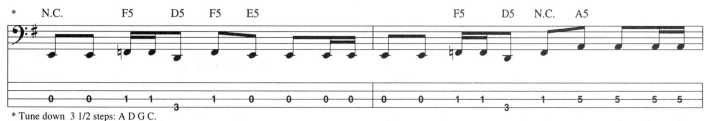

* Tune down 3 1/2 steps: A D G C.
  (This tuning simulates the bottom 4 strings of a 5-stg. bass, tuned down one whole step. For best results, instrument should be re-strung.)

Holier Than Thou

from METALLICA

Words and Music by James Hetfield and Lars Ulrich
Copyright © 1991 Creeping Death Music (ASCAP)
This Arrangement Copyright © 1992 by Creeping Death Music
International Copyright Secured All Rights Reserved

Relentless Intro Riff

A perfect example of the power of holding notes over the bar line, this riff pushes forward with great brutality. Notice how the accented notes on beat 4½ balance—and uplift— the ponderous reverse gallop figures on beats 2 and 4.

`0:00`

The Unforgiven

from METALLICA

Words and Music by James Hetfield, Lars Ulrich and Kirk Hammett
Copyright © 1991 Creeping Death Music (ASCAP)
This Arrangement Copyright © 1992 by Creeping Death Music
International Copyright Secured All Rights Reserved

Verse Riff

While Hetfield's A Dorian–based (A B C D E F♯ G) guitar part closely follows his vocal line, Newsted's part begins as a somewhat independent line, outlining the implied chord changes, until the last five bars, where it is in unison with the ensemble figures played by the guitars and drums. Play the first two sixteenth-note pull-off figures in 7th position, and the final one in 5th position.

`0:56`

Chorus Riff

Continuing his supportive role, Newsted outlines the chord progression with added passing tones, neighbor tones, as well as octave leaps—a nod to his Motown influences, particularly session-giant James Jamerson.

1:36

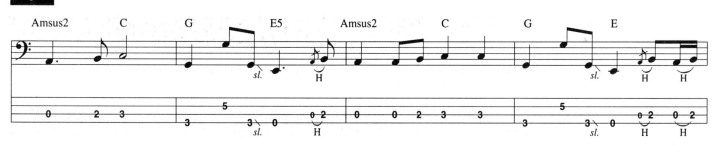

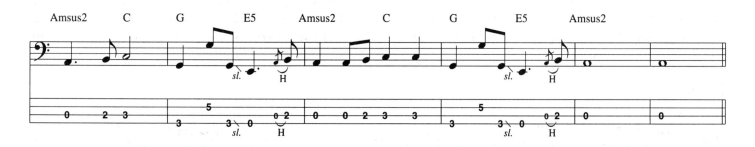

The Unforgiven (cont.)

Post-Solo Riff

This riff occurs just after Hammett's solo. Though most of this figure is in line with the approach of the previous riffs, it has some gymnastic passage work (matching the rhythm of Ulrich's fill) in the second bar; this part of the riff opens by outlining an Am7 chord, but finishes with an ornamental figure that leads into the C in bar 3.

Outro Variation

The progression used at the end of this song is essentially the same as the one used in the chorus. Compare and contrast Newsted's approach in this version with the original chorus riff (at 1:36). Try to compose your own variations on the Am–C–G–E chord progression.

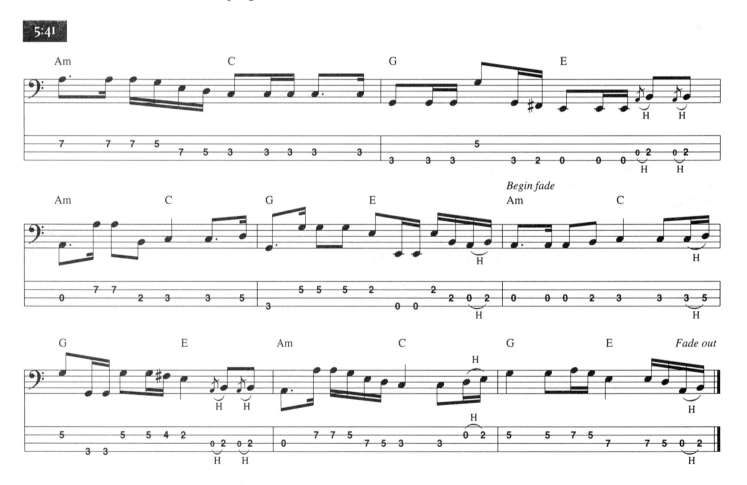

58

Wherever I May Roam

from METALLICA

Words and Music by James Hetfield and Lars Ulrich

Half-Time Riff

An improvisational feel is generated from the tremendous rhythmic variety Newsted applies here: only bars 5 and 7 contain the same rhythm.

Don't Tread On Me

from METALLICA

Words and Music by James Hetfield and Lars Ulrich

Intro Riff

Though notated in $\frac{12}{8}$ you can count this riff in 4 with a triplet feel: **1**-&-a-**2**-&-a-**3**-&-a-**4**-&-a. A back-beat feel is achieved here by using slides as an accenting device on beats **2** and **4**.

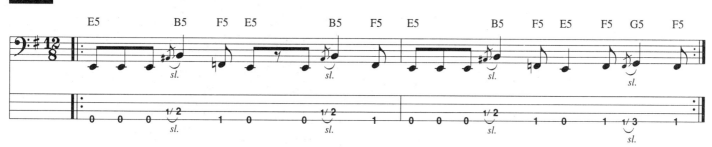

Don't Tread On Me (Cont.)

Verse-Ending Riff

This pedal-point riff is heard just before the chorus. The threes-grouped-in-twos figure in the last bar is an example of *hemiola*, a rhythmic device common in classical music since the 1400s.

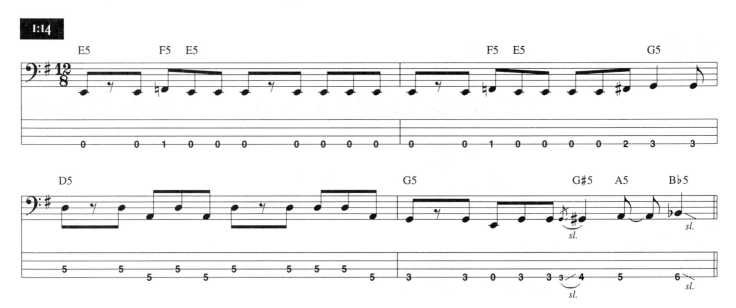

Chorus Riff

Because Hetfield's part consists mostly of straight-forward power chords (root and 5th), Newsted adds the harmonic and rhythmic twists in this section. For example, the guitars are playing an E5 chord in bars 1 and 2, but Newsted imparts a Phrygian flavor by including F♮'s in his line, and in bar 3 he establishes a rhythmic motive in the first two beats, but adds an unforeseen change on beat 4.

Through The Never

from METALLICA

Words and Music by James Hetfield, Lars Ulrich and Kirk Hammett

Intro Riff

Though most of this song is in E minor, the intro riff is in F# minor (with abundant ♭2's [G♮] and ♭5's [C♮]), which foreshadows the chorus, also in F# minor.

Nothing Else Matters

from METALLICA

Words and Music by James Hetfield and Lars Ulrich

Verse Riff

Newsted is always concerned with the finer points of his tone production—particularly on ballads; instead of playing the descending line (E–D–C) exclusively on the A string, he plays the final C on the E string, getting a warmer and darker tone than would be possible on the A string's 3rd fret C.

Nothing Else Matters (Cont.)

Chorus Riff

Ulrich is playing off the rhythms heard in the guitars, so Newsted assumes a strong, time-keeping role by laying down solid and clear rhythms—evidenced by the consecutive eighth notes in bars 1, 3, and 5, and the emphasis of the strong beats in bars 2 and 4.

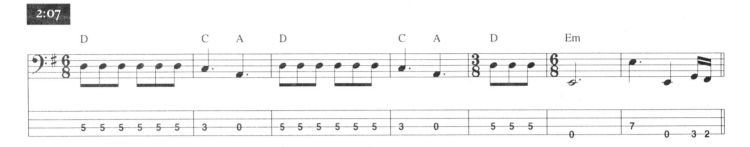

The God That Failed

from METALLICA

Words and Music by James Hetfield and Lars Ulrich

Verse Riff

Newsted's pickstyle approach enables him to use palm-muting techniques like guitarist do. Keep your hand in its normal picking position, but rest it on the strings, very close to the bridge. By keeping your palm close to the bridge, a muted tone with accurate and recognizable pitch will sound. Resting too heavily, or too closely, to the bridge can result in the pitch going sharp. Resting too far from the bride can result in the lack of a distinct pitch or can even generate harmonics.

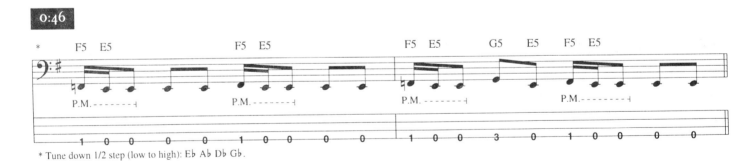

* Tune down 1/2 step (low to high): Eb Ab Db Gb.

Solo Riff

This is Newsted's accompaniment to Hammett's entire solo. Though most of this bass line has an improvisational flair, largely due to the extended sixteenth-note runs, the hits in bars 5 and 9 were certainly worked out beforehand.

2:44

* Tune down a 1/2 step (low to high): Eb Ab Db Gb.

My Friend Of Misery

from METALLICA

Words and Music by James Hetfield, Lars Ulrich and Jason Newsted
Copyright © 1991 Creeping Death Music (ASCAP)
This Arrangement Copyright © 1992 by Creeping Death Music
International Copyright Secured All Rights Reserved

Solo Bass Intro Riff

There are three things to remember when playing this intro. First, keep the tempo steady. Second, play *legato* (connected)—in fact, let all notes ring as long as possible. Third, always be conscious of the melody, which lies on the G string throughout.

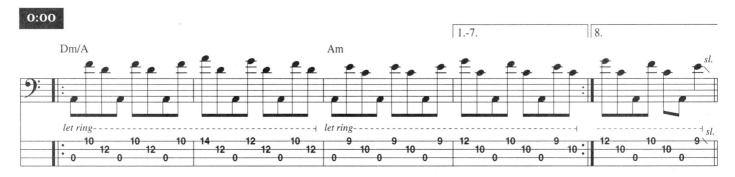

Ain't My Bitch

from LOAD

Words and Music by James Hetfield and Lars Ulrich
Copyright © 1996 Creeping Death Music (ASCAP)
This Arrangement Copyright © 1996 by Creeping Death Music
International Copyright Secured All Rights Reserved

Chorus Riff

The sixteenth notes at the end of first two bars in Newsted's part give an added push to Hetfield's syncopated vocal line.

* Tune down a 1/2 step (low to high): Eb Ab Db Gb.

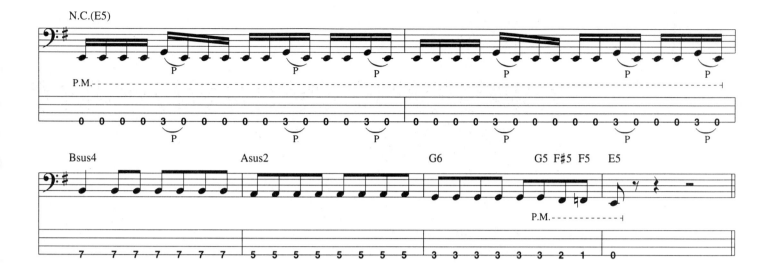

Slide-Guitar Solo Accompaniment

This solo section, in F♯ minor, follows a long section of an E pedal. The sudden and surprising jump to the new key is unified with the previous section by the rhythmic pattern ♫ ♫♫ ♫♫♫, present in both riffs.

2:43

* Tune down a 1/2 step (low to high): E♭ A♭ D♭ G♭.

Ain't My Bitch (Cont.)

2X4

from LOAD

Words and Music by James Hetfield, Lars Ulrich and Kirk Hammett

Copyright © 1996 Creeping Death Music (ASCAP)
This Arrangement Copyright © 1996 by Creeping Death Music
International Copyright Secured All Rights Reserved

Demonic Boogie Riff

This riff enters just after the drum fill and is composed of notes from the E blues scale (E G A B♭ B D). The triplets give it a boogie feel, while the prevalent B♭'s impart a demonic edge.

0:04

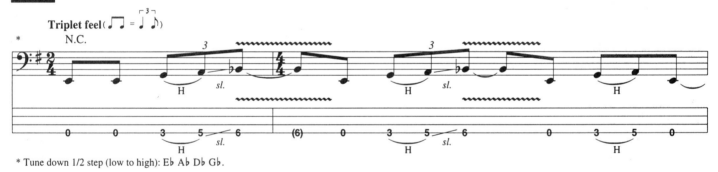

* Tune down 1/2 step (low to high): E♭ A♭ D♭ G♭.

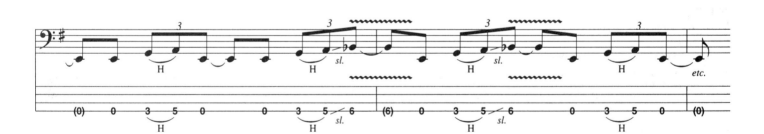

The House Jack Built

from *LOAD*

Words and Music by James Hetfield, Lars Ulrich and Kirk Hammett

Bridge Riff

If the rhythm of the sixteenth-note triplet in the first bar is difficult for you, notice that the first note of the figure falls on the "and" of beat 1, and that the 7th-fret E falls on beat 2. Work on those notes first, then let the hammer-ons fill in the space.

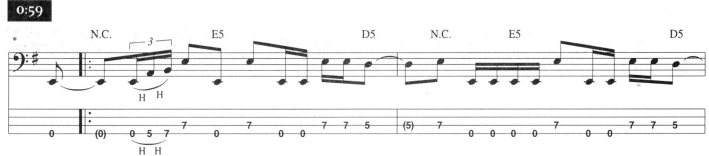

* Tune down a 1/2 step (low to high): Eb Ab Db Gb.

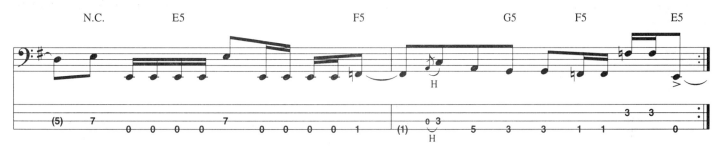

Double-Stop Riff

Other than the octave difference, this riff is identical to the guitar part—right down to the tritone double-stops. The ascending sixteenth-note figure that ends this riff should be played with one finger, either the first or second— the choice is up to you.

* Tune down a 1/2 step (low to high): Eb Ab Db Gb.

67

The House Jack Built (Cont.)

Chorus Riff

The most important—and challenging—thing about this riff is the way that it works with the drums. Lars takes a John Bonham–style approach to this ⅜ section by playing in 4/4, while Newsted and Hetfield chug away in ¾.

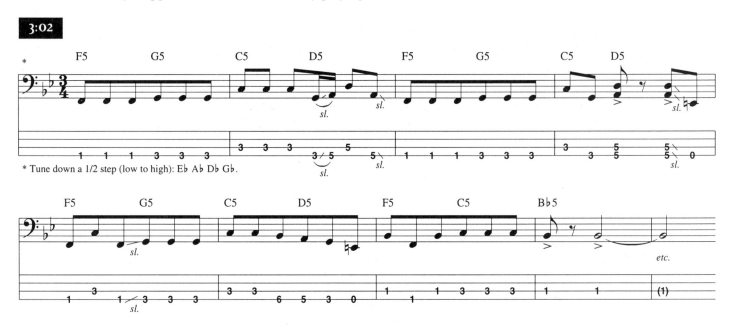

* Tune down a 1/2 step (low to high): Eb Ab Db Gb.

Until It Sleeps

from *LOAD*

Words and Music by James Hetfield and Lars Ulrich
Copyright © 1996 Creeping Death Music (ASCAP)
This Arrangement Copyright © 1996 by Creeping Death Music
International Copyright Secured All Rights Reserved

Intro/Verse Riff

Newsted plays this expressive figure on a fretless bass, but it will sound fine played on a fretted bass, if you pay careful attention to the slides.

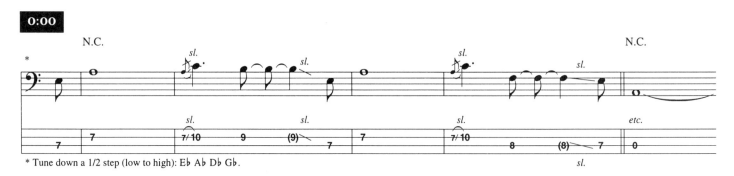

* Tune down a 1/2 step (low to high): Eb Ab Db Gb.

Chorus Riff

This riff is Newsted's take on the quintessential classic-rock progression, Am-G-F.

0:25

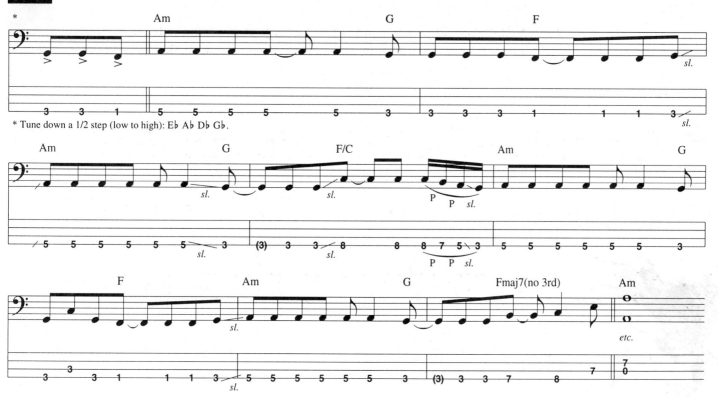

* Tune down a 1/2 step (low to high): Eb Ab Db Gb.

Bridge Riff

Nearly constant pedal point, dissonant double-stops . . . what more could Newsted do to thicken this section?

1:25

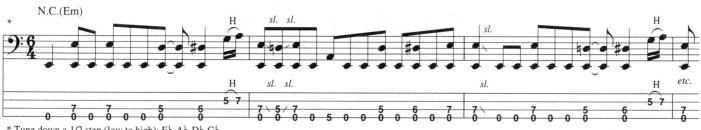

* Tune down a 1/2 step (low to high): Eb Ab Db Gb.

King Nothing

from *LOAD*

Words and Music by James Hetfield, Lars Ulrich and Kirk Hammett
Copyright © 1996 Creeping Death Music (ASCAP)
This Arrangement Copyright © 1996 by Creeping Death Music
International Copyright Secured All Rights Reserved

Intro Riff

This riff, with its funky, 1970s-style octave displacements (at the end of bars 2 and 4) is played mostly in 5th position. All of the A-string slides are played with the third finger.

* Tune down a 1/2 step (low to high): Eb Ab Db Gb.

Hero Of The Day

from *LOAD*

Words and Music by James Hetfield, Lars Ulrich and Kirk Hammett
Copyright © 1996 Creeping Death Music (ASCAP)
This Arrangement Copyright © 1996 by Creeping Death Music
International Copyright Secured All Rights Reserved

Verse Riff

This is Newsted's two-part bass line. The downstemmed part is an A pedal, and the upstemmed part is a stepwise melodic line that reflects the movement of the lowest voice of the guitar part.

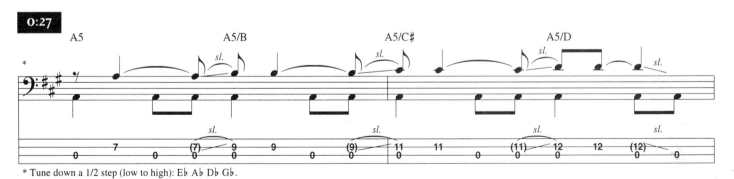

* Tune down a 1/2 step (low to high): Eb Ab Db Gb.

Heavy Chorus Riff

Perhaps it was impossible for the classic-rock vibe to last throughout the song, because here in the chorus things take a turn down a familiar Metallica alley—evidenced by a steady sixteenth-note, F# Phrygian (F# G A B C# D E) riff in the bass, a syncopated guitar part, and Ulrich's double-bass drumming.

* Tune down a 1/2 step (low to high): Eb Ab Db Gb.

Bleeding Me

from LOAD

Words and Music by James Hetfield, Lars Ulrich and Kirk Hammett

Verse Riff

Newsted plays a free-sounding part in this section that emphasizes the E minor quality.

* Tune down a 1/2 step (low to high): Eb Ab Db Gb.

Bleeding Me (Cont.)

Double-Stop Riff

Newsted uses octaves and 5ths for a meaty ending to the verse. Nearly all of the slides are played with the first finger.

1:24

* Tune down a 1/2 step (low to high): Eb Ab Db Gb.

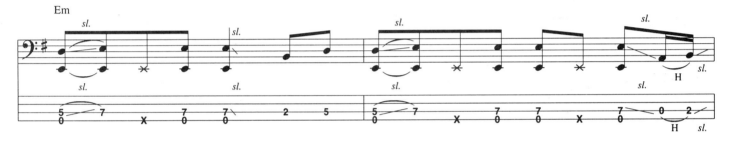

Chorus Riff

Double-stops continue to prevail in this section. Here, Newsted plays 5ths in the E5 and A5 bars, and 4ths in the D5/A bars.

2:45

* Tune down a 1/2 step (low to high): Eb Ab Db Gb.

Cure

from *LOAD*

Words and Music by James Hetfield and Lars Ulrich

Copyright © 1996 Creeping Death Music (ASCAP)
This Arrangement Copyright © 1996 by Creeping Death Music
International Copyright Secured All Rights Reserved

E Locrian Riff

The frequent emphasis of the F (♭2) and B♭ (♭5) that riddle this riff points to the E Locrian (E F G A B♭ C D) mode. The bulk of the riff is played in 1st position, so the slide from the 1st-fret B♭ into the 8th-fret F should be taken your first finger.

0:49

* Tune down a 1/2 step (low to high): E♭ A♭ D♭ G♭.

Chorus Riff

This riff is based on a rhythm from the verse (♪♫ ♫♪). Despite its velocity, Newsted plays this riff with his thumb instead of a pick.

2:09

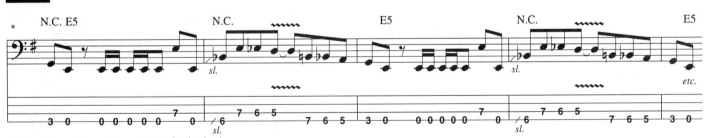

* Tune down a 1/2 step (low to high): E♭ A♭ D♭ G♭.

73

Poor Twisted Me

from *LOAD*

Words and Music by James Hetfield and Lars Ulrich

Call And Response Riff

This riff is split into two nearly identical parts (only the final note is different). Notice that the first half sounds like a question and the second half sounds like its answer.

* Tune down a 1/2 step (low to high): Eb Ab Db Gb.

Wasting My Hate

from *LOAD*

Words and Music by James Hetfield, Lars Ulrich and Kirk Hammett

Final Intro Riff

Many players put off position changes until the last possible moment; but often a position change can be made easier by changing *before* it is absolutely necessary. Try this preparatory exercise. Play the 5th-fret A on the E string with your first finger, then play it again, but this time with your third finger. Repeat the A several times using this finger switching idea. A practical application of this valuable position-changing technique occurs in the middle of bar 3.

* Tune down a 1/2 step (low to high): Eb Ab Db Gb.

Mama Said

from *LOAD*

Words and Music by James Hetfield and Lars Ulrich
Copyright © 1996 Creeping Death Music (ASCAP)
This Arrangement Copyright © 1996 by Creeping Death Music
International Copyright Secured All Rights Reserved

Chorus Riff

This melodic chorus is reminiscent of some of the acoustic songs from *Led Zeppelin III*. The 32nd-note slide in the penultimate bar should match the grace note in the vocal line.

* Tune down a 1/2 step (low to high): E♭ A♭ D♭ G♭.

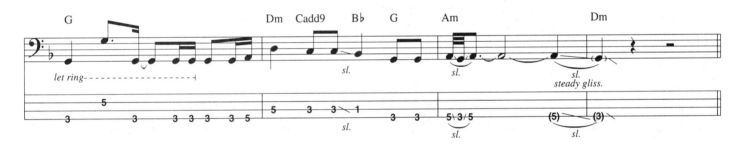

Bridge Riff

As with many other slow songs, Newsted fills the bottom end of this section with a busy sixteenth-note line. The 1st-position F major arpeggio (C–A–F) in the second bar requires some considerable finger stretching, so practice getting a clear sound on it before tackling the whole riff. The other challenging aspect of this riff is the pull-off that occurs later in the same bar. When pulling off to an open string, bring your finger down to rest on the next string. This "follow through" will ensure a strong-sounding pull-off while preventing the adjacent string from sounding accidentally.

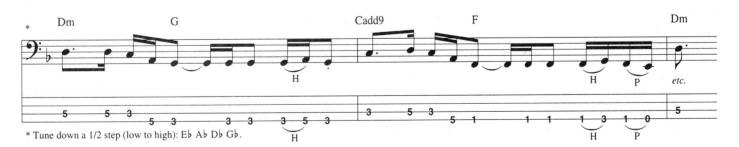

* Tune down a 1/2 step (low to high): E♭ A♭ D♭ G♭.

Thorn Within

Words and Music by James Hetfield, Lars Ulrich and Kirk Hammett
Copyright © 1996 Creeping Death Music (ASCAP)
This Arrangement Copyright © 1996 by Creeping Death Music
International Copyright Secured All Rights Reserved

Main Riff

At a glance, the first half of this riff looks easier than the second half. Not true. The odd-grouping found here can make this riff quite challenging, especially if its pattern goes unnoticed. The guitar riff is based on low F♯'s, which occur in a ♩. ♪ ♩ ♩|♩♩. ♩. ♪| rhythm. Newsted's bass line has contains this same syncopated outline, but it is "filled in" with the three-note pattern F♯–F♯–E.

0:45

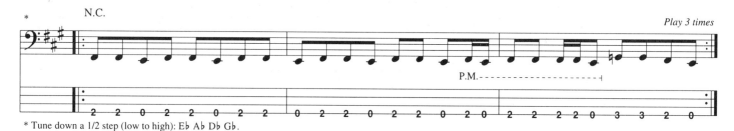

* Tune down a 1/2 step (low to high): E♭ A♭ D♭ G♭.

Ronnie

Words and Music by James Hetfield and Lars Ulrich
Copyright © 1996 Creeping Death Music (ASCAP)
This Arrangement Copyright © 1996 by Creeping Death Music
International Copyright Secured All Rights Reserved

Bluesy Intro Riff

The **x**'s in this riff represent muted notes. Play them using an downstroke, while lightly dampening the string with the left hand. The bends mimic the guitar's bends and add a bluesy touch—especially the C to C♯ bend in the second bar.

0:22

* Tune down a 1/2 step (low to high): E♭ A♭ D♭ G♭.

Final Intro Riff

This riff occurs just before the verses. The octaves and position changes encountered here make this riff fun to play. Begin in 5th position with your third finger on the 7th fret A, then move to 2nd position on beat 4 in anticipation of the pull-off figure. The final bar of the riff is played in 1st position.

0:45

* Tune down a 1/2 step (low to high): Eb Ab Db Gb.

The Outlaw Torn

from *LOAD*

Words and Music by James Hetfield and Lars Ulrich

Intro Riff

This is the riff that Newsted uses as the basis for his subtle variations on the E5–D progression. The first note of bar 2 is *pre-bent;* in other words, it is bent before it is struck.

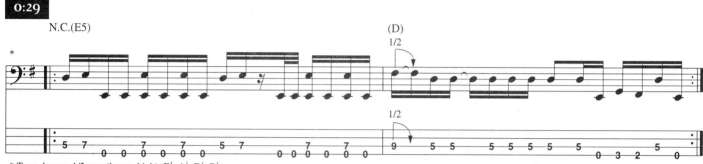

* Tune down a 1/2 step (low to high): E♭ A♭ D♭ B♭.

Verse Riff

Newsted's bass line is the only pitched accompaniment for Hetfield's vocal, so he keeps things moving by outlining an Em chord and using vibrant rhythms.

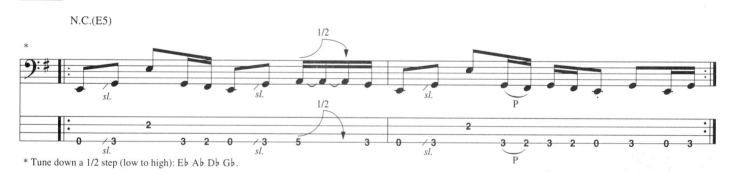

* Tune down a 1/2 step (low to high): E♭ A♭ D♭ G♭.

Chorus Riff

The intro riff is brought to new heights in this section of the verse. The tempo is slow, so don't panic over all the 32nd notes. Compare this riff to the simpler version found in the intro.

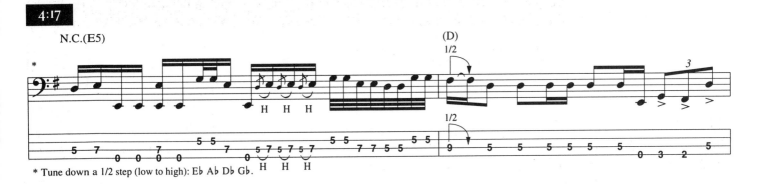

* Tune down a 1/2 step (low to high): Eb Ab Db Gb.

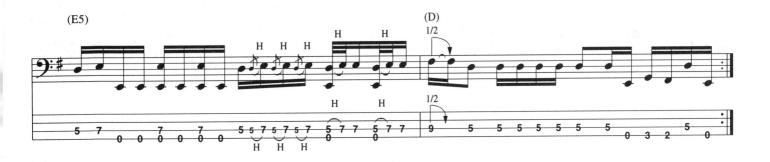

___

About The Author...

Arthur Rotfeld is a guitarist, composer, and arranger. He received bachelor degrees in education and jazz studies from The University of Bridgeport, and earned a Master of Fine Arts in composition from SUNY Purchase, where he also taught solfège. Arthur has also taught in public schools, and as a private instructor of guitar, bass, and piano. Other titles by Arthur include *The Art of Kirk Hammett, Soundgarden Riff by Riff,* and *Slayer Riff by Riff.* Arthur lives in White Plains, N.Y. and performs regularly in the New York metropolitan area.

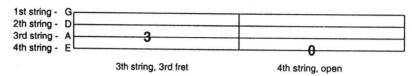

BASS TABLATURE EXPLANATION/NOTATION LEGEND

Bass tablature is a four-line staff that graphically represents the bass fingerboard. By placing a number on the appropriate line, the string and fret of any note can be indicated. The number 0 represents an open string. For example:

```
1st string - G
2th string - D
3rd string - A          3
4th string - E                        0
```

3th string, 3rd fret   4th string, open

Definitions for Special Bass Notation (for both traditional and tablature bass lines)

BEND: Strike the note and bend up 1/2 step (one fret).

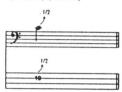

BEND: Strike the note and bend up a whole step (two frets).

BEND AND RELEASE: Strike the note. Bend up 1/2 (or whole) step, then release the bend back to the original note. All three notes are tied; only the first note is struck.

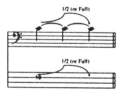

PRE-BEND: Bend the note up 1/2 (or whole) step, then strike it.

PRE-BEND AND RELEASE: Bend the note up 1/2 (or whole) step. Strike it and release the bend back to the original note.

VIBRATO: Vibrate the note by rapidly bending and releasing it with the left hand.

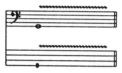

SLIDE: Strike the first note and then with the same left-hand finger move up the string to the location of the second note. The second note is not struck.

SLIDE: Same as above, except the second note is struck.

SLIDE: Slide up to the note indicated from a few frets below.

SLIDE: Strike the note and slide up an indefinite number of frets, releasing finger pressure at the end of the slide.

HAMMER-ON: Strike the first (lower) note, then sound the higher note with another finger by fretting it without picking.

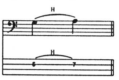

PULL-OFF: Place both fingers on the notes to be sounded. Strike the first (higher) note, then sound the lower note by pulling the finger off the higher note while keeping the lower note fretted.

TAPPING: Hammer ("tap") the fret indicated with the right-hand index or middle finger and pull off to the note fretted by the left hand ("T" indicates "tapped" notes).

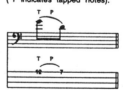

NATURAL HARMONIC: With a left-hand finger, lightly touch the string over the fret indicated, then strike it. A chime-like sound is produced.

ARTIFICIAL HARMONIC: Fret the note normally and sound the harmonic by lightly touching the node point on the string with the edge of the right-hand thumb while simultaneously plucking with the right-hand index or middle finger.

PALM MUTE: If using a pick, partially mute the note by lightly touching the string with the right hand just before the bridge.

SLAP AND POP: Slap (▼) the string with the side of the thumb. Pop (◑) or snap the string with the index or middle finger by pulling and releasing it so that it rebounds against the fretboard.

MUFFLED STRING: Lay the left hand across the string without depressing it to the fretboard. Strike the string with the right hand, producing a percussive sound.